World Book's Documenting History
World War II in the Pacific

WORLD
BOOK

a Scott Fetzer company
Chicago

www.worldbookonline.com

World Book, Inc.
233 N. Michigan Avenue
Chicago, IL 60601
U.S.A.

For information about other World Book publications, visit our Web site at **http://www.worldbookonline.com** or call **1-800-WORLDBK (967-5325)**.

For information about sales to schools and libraries, call **1-800-975-3250 (United States)**, or **1-800-837-5365 (Canada)**.

Library of Congress Cataloging-in-Publication Data

World War II in the Pacific.
   p. cm. -- (World Book's documenting history)
   Summary: "A history of World War II as it was fought in the Pacific, based on primary source documents and other historical artifacts. Features include period art works and photographs; excerpts from literary works, letters, speeches, broadcasts, and diaries; summary boxes; a timeline; maps; and a list of additional resources"-- Provided by publisher.
   Includes bibliographical references and index.
   ISBN 978-0-7166-1510-1
   1. World War, 1939-1945--Pacific Area--Juvenile literature.
   2. World War, 1939-1945--Pacific Area--Sources--Juvenile literature.
   I. World Book, Inc. II. Title: World War 2 in the Pacific. III. Title: World War Two in the Pacific.
   D767.W64 2010
   940.54'26--dc22
                        2010008910

World Book's Documenting History
Set ISBN 978-0-7166-1498-2
Printed in Malaysia by TWP Sdn Bhd, JohorBahru
1st printing September 2010

Contents

The Axis Powers

Whe n World War II began with Nazi Germany's invasion of Poland on Sept. 1, 1939, Germany's allies Japan and Italy were already at war. Japan had invaded Manchuria—a region in China—in 1931. In 1937, Japan invaded the rest of China. Italy had invaded Ethiopia in eastern Africa in 1935 and Albania in southern Europe in 1939.

Germany, Italy, and Japan were known as the Axis powers. By 1941, the Axis powers had conquered most of Europe, much of North Africa and Southeast Asia, and many Pacific islands. Defending against Axis aggression were the Allies—originally just France, the United Kingdom, and such British Commonwealth nations as Australia and Canada. In June 1941, Germany attacked the Soviet Union. That attack caused the Soviets to join the Allies. In December 1941, the Americans joined the Allies after Japan's attack upon the United States at Pearl Harbor, Hawaii.

▶ The Tripartite Pact—a treaty between Germany, Italy, and Japan—was signed on Sept. 27, 1940.

▼ The signing of the Tripartite Pact in Berlin, Germany. The Japanese ambassador (left) stands, holding the document. Seated (center) is the Italian foreign minister and (right) German dictator Adolf Hitler (1889-1945). The Tripartite Pact created the Axis powers.

ARTICLE ONE: Japan recognizes . . . the leadership of Germany and Italy in the establishment of a new order in Europe.

ARTICLE TWO: Germany and Italy recognize . . . the leadership of Japan in the establishment of a new order in greater East Asia.

ARTICLE THREE: Germany, Italy, and Japan . . . undertake to assist one another with all . . . means when one of the three . . . is attacked. . . .

from the Tripartite Pact, 1940

3

. . . For on Sept. 27th, 1940, this year, by an agreement signed in Berlin, three powerful nations . . . joined themselves together in the threat that if the United States of America interfered with or blocked the *expansion* [growth] program of these three nations—a program aimed at world control—they would unite . . . against the United States . . . there is far less chance of the United States getting into war if we do all we can now to support the nations defending themselves against attack by the Axis than if we . . . *submit* [give in] tamely to an Axis victory, and wait our turn to be the object of attack in another war later on.

Franklin D. Roosevelt

◀ A radio broadcast from Dec. 29, 1940, by U.S. President Franklin D. Roosevelt (1882-1945). Roosevelt made regular radio broadcasts known as "fireside chats." In this broadcast, Roosevelt expressed his belief that the Tripartite Pact posed a danger to the United States. At the time of the broadcast, Roosevelt was already secretly helping the Allies.

4

▶ Emperor Hirohito (1901-1989) of Japan inspects his troops. The Japanese emperor, also known as the Showa Emperor, was considered by the Japanese to be a god, but he did not completely control government policy for Japan. Military leaders, led by General Hideki Tojo (1884-1948), Japan's prime minister as of 1941, determined many of Japan's policies.

NOW YOU KNOW

- Germany, Italy, and Japan signed the Tripartite Act in 1940, creating the Axis powers.
- By 1941, the Axis powers ruled much of Europe, Africa, and areas of the Pacific.
- Japan's government was heavily controlled by the military.

Japanese Aggression in Asia

I N THE EARLY 1930's, THE JAPANESE EMPIRE INCLUDED KOREA, TAIWAN (known then as Formosa), many Pacific islands, and the northern Chinese region of Manchuria. In July 1937, a clash occurred between Chinese troops and Japanese troops that were stationed at the Marco Polo Bridge, near Beijing. After this incident, the Japanese sent still more troops into China. The conflict grew, and soon Japan had captured large areas of Chinese land and had killed thousands of Chinese people. Japanese troops were particularly brutal to Chinese citizens in Nanking (now Nanjing) in December 1937. The United States protested the Japanese *aggression* (unprovoked attacks) in Asia and feared for its own Pacific territories. In the summer of 1941, the U.S. government stopped the trade of most goods, including oil, with Japan.

▲ Japanese troops entering the Chinese city of Nanking in December 1937. The troops behaved with terrible cruelty toward Chinese soldiers and civilians in Nanking and other captured territories.

▶ An account in *The New York Times* describes the behavior of Japanese troops in Nanking. The American reporter F. Tillman Durdin (1907-1998) was one of the last Western journalists to leave the city. As many as 300,000 Chinese died during what became known as the "Rape of Nanking."

Two days of Japanese *occupation* [enemy troops taking possession] changed the whole outlook . . . the *violation* [rape] of women, the murder of civilians . . . mass executions of war prisoners . . . turned Nanking into a city of terror. The killing of civilians was widespread. Foreigners who traveled widely through the city Wednesday found civilians dead on every street. Some of the victims were aged men, women, and children.

The New York Times, 1937

3

In view of the unlimited national emergency declared by the President, he has today issued an *Executive* [presidential] Order freezing Japanese *assets* [things of value] in the United States. . . . This measure, in effect, brings all financial and import and export trade *transactions* [business exchanges] in which Japanese interests are involved under the control of the [U.S.] government, and imposes criminal penalties for *violation* [breaking] of the order. . . .

This Executive Order . . . is designed among other things to prevent . . . trade between Japan and the United States in ways harmful to national defense and American interests.

The New York Times, 1941

▲ In July 1941, *The New York Times* reports President Roosevelt's response to Japanese aggression in Asia. Japan had invaded France's Asian colonies—known as French Indochina (now Cambodia, Laos, and Vietnam). Roosevelt ordered Japanese assets to be frozen, preventing Japan from buying war materials from the United States, including the oil Japan needed to power its military *campaigns* (war operations).

4

▶ The "Flying Tigers," a group of volunteer American combat pilots, fought for the Chinese Air Force against Japan. They began training in China before the United States entered World War II.

NOW YOU KNOW

- Japan invaded China in the 1930's.
- Japanese troops treated the Chinese with great cruelty.
- The United States stopped the sale of oil and other important products to Japan in 1941.

Pearl Harbor

O N Dec. 7, 1941, THE JAPANESE LAUNCHED A SURPRISE ATTACK upon the U.S. Pacific Fleet at Pearl Harbor, Hawaii. Two large groups of Japanese warplanes sank several U.S. ships—all eight U.S. battleships at the harbor were destroyed or badly damaged— and destroyed more than 180 U.S. aircraft. The Japanese killed around 2,400 Americans, but they lost fewer than 100 of their own airmen. The attack initially looked like a great military success for Japan. Eventually, however, bringing the United States into the war was a disaster for the Japanese Empire and its citizens.

1

Since Japan is unavoidably facing national *ruin* [disaster] whether it decides to fight the United States or *submit* [give in] to its demands, it must by all means choose to fight. Japan would rather go down fighting than *ignobly* [without honor] surrender without a struggle, because surrender would spell spiritual as well as physical ruin for the nation and its destiny.

Admiral Osami Nagano

▲ At an imperial conference in September 1941, Japanese Navy Chief of Staff Admiral Osami Nagano (1880-1947) expresses the view that Japan needs to attack the United States. He believed that the economic penalties President Roosevelt ordered to stop Japan's aggression against other Asian nations (see page 7) would financially ruin the nation. Japanese tradition was built upon the warrior spirit. Defeat and death were preferable to dishonor, and it was thought that giving in to American demands to end the war in China would bring dishonor upon Japan.

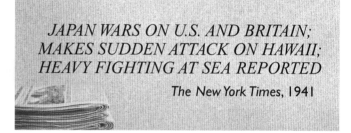

JAPAN WARS ON U.S. AND BRITAIN; MAKES SUDDEN ATTACK ON HAWAII; HEAVY FIGHTING AT SEA REPORTED

The New York Times, 1941

▲ The Dec. 8, 1941, *New York Times* headline announces the bombings at Pearl Harbor.
▼ The Japanese paper presents the Pearl Harbor attack as a knockout blow directed at a powerful, bullying foe.

2

3

Yesterday, December 7, 1941—a date which will live in *infamy* [disgrace]—the United States of America was suddenly and deliberately attacked by naval and air forces of the Empire of Japan. . . .

The attack yesterday on the Hawaiian Islands has caused severe damage to American naval and military forces. I regret to tell you that very many American lives have been lost . . . .

I, therefore, ask that the Congress declare that since the unprovoked and *dastardly* [cowardly] attack by Japan on Sunday, December 7, 1941, a state of war has existed between the United States and the Japanese Empire.

Franklin D. Roosevelt

◀ In a speech meant for both the U.S. Congress and the American people, broadcast on radio on Dec. 8, 1941, President Roosevelt expresses the outrage Americans felt at Japan's sudden attack on Pearl Harbor. Roosevelt asked Congress to declare war. That same day, Australia, Canada, and the United Kingdom also declared war on Japan. On December 11, Nazi Germany and Italy declared war on the United States; the world was at war.

4

▶ Sailors in a small boat rescue a survivor in the water during the bombing of Pearl Harbor. The line of eight battleships at port in the harbor on December 7 was known as "Battleship Row." All eight of the battleships in that row were sunk or badly damaged. One, the U.S.S. *Arizona,* went down within minutes and burned in the harbor for two days. That ship still lies at the bottom of Pearl Harbor—a tomb holding more than 1,000 crewmen who died that day.

NOW YOU KNOW

- Japanese planes attacked the U.S. Pacific Fleet at Pearl Harbor, Hawaii, on Dec. 7, 1941.
- President Franklin D. Roosevelt asked Congress to declare war on Japan on December 8.
- Germany and Italy declared war on the United States on December 11.

Southeast Asia Invaded

EIGHT HOURS AFTER THE ATTACK ON PEARL HARBOR, THE JAPANESE ATTACKED the British colony of Hong Kong on the southern coast of China and two other U.S. islands in the Pacific Ocean—Guam and Wake. (Because of the position of the International Date Line, which lies between Hawaii and Asia, the date of these attacks was Dec. 8, 1941, though the attacks occurred only hours after Pearl Harbor.) At the same time, the Japanese also invaded the Philippines and Southeast Asia, taking Thailand in just hours. Japanese forces advanced into the British-ruled regions of Malaya (now part of Malaysia) and Burma (now Myanmar), eventually advancing to the island of Singapore and forcing 60,000 British troops to surrender there on Feb. 15, 1942. The Japanese seemed unstoppable.

◀ The Japanese Empire in 1942, shown in stages of expansion from 1931. Vast areas of the Pacific were under Japanese rule by the spring of 1942.

▶ Harold Nicolson (1886-1968), a British Member of Parliament, in a diary entry from Feb. 27, 1942. Nicolson notes how shocked the British were by the fall of Singapore, the great British fortress in the East. He feared that the United Kingdom might lack the will to defend India and other parts of its empire against the dedicated and committed Japanese Empire.

This Singapore surrender has been a terrific blow to all of us. It is not merely the immediate dangers which threaten in the Indian Ocean. . . . It is the dread that we are only half-hearted in fighting the whole-hearted.

Harold Nicolson

3

◀ *The Sphere*, a British magazine, describes and illustrates the sinking of the British ships the *Repulse* and the *Prince of Wales* on Dec. 10, 1941. These powerful warships had just arrived in the East to defend British colonies from the Japanese. *The Sphere* correctly notes that the ships were without *air cover* (protection by aircraft).

▶ Cecil Brown (1907-1987), a war correspondent for CBS radio, describes an attack on his ship in his book *Suez to Singapore* (1942). Brown was on the *Repulse* and survived to record the sinking of the battleship. The *Prince of Wales* sank in the same battle. Brown had thought it "impossible" for aircraft to destroy such mighty ships. The sinkings of these British ships showed the importance of aircraft to the war at sea.

4

The torpedo strikes the ship about 20 yards [18 meters] *astern* [at the rear of a ship] of my position. It feels as though the ship has crashed into dock. I am thrown 4 feet [1.3 meters] across the deck . . . . Almost immediately, it seems, the ship *lists* [leans to one side] . . . the *Repulse* is going down . . . . The torpedo-smashed *Prince of Wales* . . . is low in the water . . . . Japanese bombers are still *winging* [flying] around like vultures . . . . My mind cannot *absorb* [take in] what my eyes see. It is impossible that these two beautiful, powerful, *invulnerable* [unsinkable] ships are going down. But they are.

Cecil Brown

NOW YOU KNOW

- The Japanese won many early victories in Southeast Asia and the Pacific.
- Around 60,000 British troops surrendered at Singapore.
- It became clear that air power would be a major factor in the war.

The Fall of the Philippines

JAPAN LANDED TROOPS IN THE PHILIPPINES ON DEC. 8, 1941. American and Philippine forces, under U.S. Army General Douglas MacArthur (1880-1964), defended the islands. However, MacArthur's forces soon abandoned Manila, the capital, and withdrew to the nearby Bataan Peninsula. In March, MacArthur was ordered to leave for Australia, and General Jonathan M. Wainwright (1883-1953) took over the command. Although suffering from hunger and disease, the Allied forces beat back Japanese attacks until April 9, 1942, when they surrendered at Bataan. Some Allied troops escaped and continued to fight on Corregidor, a Philippine island south of Bataan. Japanese forces landed on Corregidor on May 5. Overwhelmed, the Allies surrendered Corregidor on May 6—the Philippines had fallen.

1

. . . they [American bomber crews] rushed out in a *futile* [useless] attempt to take the big machines off. . . . One after another, these vitally needed, expensive, irreplaceable bombers collapsed in bullet-ridden heaps, or sagged to the *ravenous* [hungry] flames that were consuming them.

Captain Allison Ind

▲ In his book *Bataan: The Judgment Seat* (1944), U.S. Captain Allison Ind, an eyewitness, describes the Japanese attack on the Philippines. On Dec. 8, 1941, hours after Pearl Harbor, Japanese aircraft attacked Clark Field, a U.S. airfield in the Philippines. Americans in the Philippines knew of the attack on Pearl Harbor but were still unprepared. Most of the planes at Clark Field were destroyed on the ground.

▶ A poster urges Philippine soldiers to fight the Japanese. Philippine forces suffered higher casualties than the Americans and, as prisoners, were treated more harshly by the Japanese.

2

THE FIGHTING FILIPINOS

WE WILL ALWAYS FIGHT FOR *FREEDOM!*

3

The president of the United States ordered me to break through the Japanese lines and proceed from Corregidor to Australia for the purpose, as I understand it, of organizing the American offensive against Japan, a *primary* [main] object of which is the relief of the Philippines. I came through and I shall return.

Gen. Douglas MacArthur

◀ Speaking to reporters upon his arrival in Australia in March 1942, MacArthur promises to return to the Philippines. General MacArthur left his troops in the Philippines on a direct order from President Franklin Roosevelt. MacArthur's promise, "I shall return," became a famous symbol of Allied determination.

▼ Japanese soldiers celebrate after the capture of American *artillery* (a large gun) on the Bataan Peninsula.

4

NOW YOU KNOW

- Japanese warplanes attacked the Philippines just hours after the attack on Pearl Harbor. Japanese troops landed in the Philippines the same day.

- In March 1942, General MacArthur was ordered to leave the Philippines to take up a new command; he promised to return.

- American and Philippine forces held out on the Bataan Peninsula until April 1942.

Bataan Death March

ON APRIL 9, 1942, EXHAUSTED AMERICAN AND PHILIPPINE TROOPS on Bataan surrendered to the Japanese. Some 75,000 soldiers were taken prisoner by the Japanese. Thousands of these prisoners died of disease and mistreatment on a 65-mile (105-kilometer) forced march to prison camps—the Bataan Death March. Some experts estimate that as many as one out of every four prisoners died on the march. They were denied food and water and were treated with great cruelty by the Japanese. Many were executed.

► Japanese soldiers force surrendering American and Philippine troops to pose for a photograph taken on Bataan in 1942. The Japanese treated the prisoners with great brutality on the Bataan Death March.

The hours dragged by and . . . the dropouts began . . . a great many of the prisoners reached the end of their *endurance* [ability to go on]. . . . Usually, they made an effort to rise . . . . Some succeeded. Others lay lifelessly where they had fallen. . . . There was a sharp crackle of pistol and rifle fire behind us . . . a hundred yards [90 meters] behind our *contingent* [group], came a "clean-up squad" of murdering Jap buzzards. Their helpless victims . . . were easy targets. . . . The bodies were left where they lay, that other prisoners coming behind us might see them.

Captain William Dyess

◄ Captain William "Ed" Dyess (1916-1943), an American fighter pilot who survived the Bataan Death March, describes the terrible treatment of prisoners by some of the Japanese soldiers. In 1943, Dyess managed to escape the prisoner of war (POW) camp in the Philippines at which he was held. Upon his return to the United States, he told his story to the *Chicago Tribune*. Only after his death did the U.S. government permit the story to be published in the *Tribune* and in a book, *The Dyess Story* (1944).

3

The Imperial Japanese Forces . . . are going well out of their way to feed and help 50,000 men who once were their enemies. . . . If, in spite of the *humane* [kind] treatment the Japanese are giving these prisoners, the latter are too weak to reach their destinations, we have only the high command of the American forces to blame for surrendering when many of their men had already been terribly weakened by lack of food and by diseases.

The Tribune, 1942

◀ *The Tribune*, a Manila newspaper under Japanese control, claims that the Japanese are treating their prisoners well. The writer blames the Americans for their own suffering. The even larger number of Philippine people who died on the march is not mentioned at all, as the Japanese did not want to further anger the Philippine population.

4

▶ A telegram sent by the U.S. War Department to the *Seattle Post-Intelligencer* tries to give hope to the wives and mothers of Americans captured on Bataan. The telegram suggests that Japanese leaders will improve prison-camp conditions, but this did not come to pass.

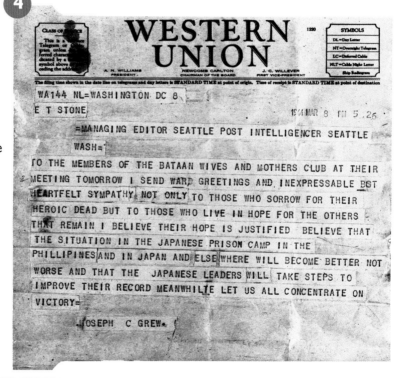

NOW YOU KNOW

- Around 75,000 Allied soldiers were taken prisoner by the Japanese on Bataan Peninsula on April 9, 1942.

- Thousands of these prisoners died on the Bataan Death March.

- The Japanese treated the Philippine soldiers worse than they treated the Americans.

Women in the War

IN THE SOVIET UNION, MANY WOMEN FOUGHT IN FRONT-LINE INFANTRY, tank, and air-combat units. In the other Allied countries, women were not given combat roles, but they did work in shipyards and aircraft factories and filled many jobs previously held only by men. Many women worked as military nurses or served in armed forces such as the U.S. Women's Army Corps (WAC). Despite the fact that women were not meant to be in combat, women in several types of jobs, especially nursing, were often at or near the front. With the fall of the Philippines, nearly 80 Allied nurses became prisoners of war (POW's). Near the end of the war, women in Japan had begun to work in industry because of the shortage of men in that country.

1

[Ann Bernatitus] On April 7, the following week, they bombed us again. It was terrible. . . . On the 8th, we were transferred to Corregidor. That's when the *front lines* [place where two opposing armies meet] collapsed.

[Interviewer] What did you see when you looked across at Bataan?

[Bernatitus] Fireworks. You wouldn't believe. They [the Japanese] had bombs and everything. . . . I was less scared on Bataan than I was on Corregidor. When the Japanese bombed, the whole place just shook . . . . We were in the hospital tunnel. . . . The main tunnel was where [generals] MacArthur and Wainwright had their headquarters.

Ann Bernatitus

◀ U.S. Navy nurse Ann Bernatitus (1912-2003) recalls looking after the sick and wounded on Bataan and Corregidor in 1942, in an interview with a Navy historian in 1994. The nurses in the Philippines became known as "Angels of Bataan." Many of those nurses became Japanese prisoners of war. Bernatitus was with the last group of Americans that escaped before Corregidor fell. Bernatitus received a medal, the Legion of Merit, for her bravery in the Philippines.

2

We *thrived* [did well] on the hard work. Being in the message center . . . we knew pretty much what was going on and how important our work was. We would know, for example, that a big landing was about to take place. . . . The tension was *palpable* [easy to feel]. The message traffic got *frantic* [very excited], as the job of getting troops, supplies, and ships all together . . . drew to a close. Then one morning we looked out to sea; where yesterday there had been hundreds of ships, today there was not a one.

Selene Weise

▶ Selene Weise (1917-2010), in her book *The Good Soldier* (1999), describes the communications work performed by women in the Signal Corps. Weise was stationed in New Guinea and the Philippines in 1944 when both were combat zones.

3

▲ Admiral Thomas Kinkaid (1888-1972) greets nurses that had been held as prisoners of war after the fall of the Philippines. The nurses were rescued in February 1945; they had been held prisoner for nearly three years.

NOW YOU KNOW

- Most nations did not allow women to serve in combat.
- Women worked in factories and served as nurses and in support roles in the armed forces.
- Many nurses became prisoners of war following the fall of the Philippines.

The Conquest of Burma

JAPANESE FORCES ADVANCED INTO SOUTHERN BURMA in December 1941. China sent troops to help the United Kingdom's Burma Corps to hold a supply route to China called the Burma Road. Weapons, food, and other goods traveled over the Burma Road. In April 1942, Japan seized and shut the road down. The Japanese fought skillfully in difficult conditions, and by mid-May they had driven Allied forces from most of Burma. The Chinese were forced to withdraw, and the British made a painful 1,000-mile (1,600-kilometer) retreat to India.

1

The Japanese fought with great *ferocity* [fierceness] and courage. We were *arrogant* [too proud] about the *Japs* [an insulting term for the Japanese]—we regarded them as *coolies* [laborers]. We thought of them as third-rate. My goodness, we soon changed our tune. We had no idea about jungle fighting. . . .

John Randle

◀ In an interview, British officer John Randle describes the effect of racial prejudice on Allied thinking. The British had underestimated the courage and skill of the Japanese soldier. The interview with Randle was recorded by London's Imperial War Museum and later published in the book *Forgotten Voices of World War II* (2004).

▶ In his book *Defeat into Victory* (1956), British General William Slim (1891-1970) describes the difference in attitude and training between the British and the Japanese concerning warfare in the jungle.

2

To our men, British or Indian, the jungle was a strange, fearsome place; moving and fighting in it were a nightmare. We were too ready to classify jungle as *"impenetrable"* [not able to be entered], as indeed it was to us with our motor transport, bulky supplies, and inexperience. To us it appeared only as an obstacle to movement and to vision; to the Japanese it was a welcome means of concealed *manoeuvre* [the British spelling of maneuver] and surprise.

General William Slim

▼ Japanese *infantry* (foot soldiers) cross a river. The soldiers walk on a bamboo footbridge supported by other soldiers. Japanese forces had an impressive ability to solve problems without the help of advanced technology, which aided them in the kind of warfare they faced in Burma.

NOW YOU KNOW

- The Burma Road was an important Allied supply route.
- The British were ill-prepared for jungle fighting.
- The Japanese eventually drove the Allies from Burma.

The Battle of the Java Sea

IN JANUARY 1942, THE JAPANESE BEGAN A RAPID OCCUPATION of the oil-rich Netherlands East Indies (now Indonesia). Although weakened by earlier naval losses, the Allies hoped to save the East Indian island of Java by stopping the Japanese at sea. The Allies combined their remaining forces into the American, British, Dutch, and Australian (ABDA) fleet. As Japanese invasion convoys approached Java, Dutch admiral Karel Doorman (1889-1942) led five cruisers and nine destroyers into action. The Allies were outnumbered and outgunned and, since the Allied ships and crews came from four different navies, they were not a well-unified force. The Battle of the Java Sea on February 27 was an easy Japanese victory. More than 2,000 Allied sailors were killed—including Admiral Doorman—and five Allied ships were sunk. Java and the rest of the Netherlands East Indies fell to Japan in early March.

▲ The light cruiser *De Ruyter* before the Battle of the Java Sea. Dutch Admiral Karel Doorman was the commander of the Allied fleet at the battle. Doorman and most of his crew went down with the *De Ruyter* when it was hit and sunk by a Japanese torpedo.

2

One of the *decisive* [having a result beyond question] sea battles of history was fought last week in the *placid* [calm] waters between Java and Borneo. It was the naval battle for Java. It was a battle for the last *bulwark* [defense] against Japanese conquest of the Indies, a battle for the Southwest Pacific, a battle for a great chunk of the world's seas and sea power. It was a battle fought too late and in the wrong place, lost before it began.

Time, 1942

◄ A March 9, 1942, story in *Time* magazine describes the Allied defeat in the Java Sea in February 1942. It was the biggest sea battle since World War I (1914-1918) and a brutal loss for the Allies.

3

► Concluding a 21-point report on the Allied losses, an Australian officer at the Battle of the Java Sea, Commodore John A. Collins (1899-1989), identifies a major Allied weakness. Naval fleets normally spend much time practicing *maneuvers* (coordinated movements) and becoming familiar with acting as a unit. The units of the ABDA fleet spoke different languages and used different signaling systems. They had no experience of working together.

21. It should be noted that throughout this action the Allied forces suffered from communication difficulties. The force as a whole had never acted before as a *tactical unit* [a group organized for a military purpose]. Visual signaling was restricted to simple signals in English by flashing lamp in Morse Code. British Liaison Officers with small signal staffs were on board [the ships] DE RUYTER and JAVA, but it had not been practicable to adopt a common system of flag signaling.

J. A. Collins

NOW YOU KNOW

• The Allies could not stop the Japanese from taking Java.

• The Battle of the Java Sea was the largest naval battle since World War I.

• Communication problems added greatly to the Allies' difficulties in this battle.

The Tide Begins to Turn

ALTHOUGH THE JAPANESE HAD CAUSED CONSIDERABLE DAMAGE at Pearl Harbor, they missed one of the real strengths of the U.S. Navy—*aircraft carriers* (large ships from which airplanes can take off and on which they can land and be stored). In May 1942, American warplanes based from aircraft carriers stopped a Japanese force in the Coral Sea, northeast of Australia. In June 1942, a large Japanese naval force attacked the U.S. military base at Midway Island in the central Pacific Ocean. However, a group of U.S. Navy aircraft carriers was waiting for them. In the Battle of Midway, American warplanes destroyed the heart of the Japanese Navy in a great Allied victory. The tide was turning.

◀ A painting by American artist Robert Benney (1904-2001) shows the destruction of the Japanese aircraft carrier *Shoho* during the Battle of the Coral Sea (May 4 through May 8). The battle was fought entirely by aircraft—the first naval battle in which enemy ships never saw or fired upon one another.

▶ In his book *Midway, the Battle that Doomed Japan* (1955), Japanese Captain Mitsuo Fuchida (1920-1976) recalls the Battle of Midway (June 4 through June 6). Fuchida was on the Japanese aircraft carrier *Akagi*. Planes being loaded with torpedoes on *Akagi*'s deck were open to attack by U.S. dive-bombers. A bomb dropped by the Americans resulted in a fire aboard the *Akagi*, which sank on June 5.

We had been caught *flatfooted* [unprepared] . . . [with] decks loaded with planes armed and fueled for attack . . . I was horrified at the destruction that had been wrought in a matter of seconds. There was a huge hole in [the surface used for planes to take off and land]. . . . Deck plates reeled upward. . . . Planes stood tail up, belching . . . flame and jet-black smoke . . . tears streamed down my cheeks as I watched the fires spread. . . .

Mitsuo Fuchida

American dive-bombers near a burning Japanese warship during the Battle of Midway. U.S. warplanes from aircraft carriers destroyed four Japanese aircraft carriers and many other ships during the four-day battle.

▶ In his book *Crossing the Line* (1994), U.S. sailor Alvin Kernan (1923-   ) describes how an aircraft-carrier crew might not know if their warplanes had succeeded until they returned—or failed to return. Naval air battles were fought over great distances.

. . . we waited for them on the deck of the [U.S. aircraft carrier] *Enterprise* . . . one, two, three, and four torpedo planes *straggled* [wandered] in separately, and that was it . . . . The loss was unimaginable . . . even when the survivors, in a condition of shock, told us what kind of slaughter it had been. . . . Within a few minutes after the first attack on the *Yorktown,* her dive-bombers and ours began arriving. . . . But now the mood was triumphant. The bomber pilots . . . were shouting and laughing as they jumped out of the cockpit, and the ship which had been so *somber* [sad] . . . became now hysterically excited.

Alvin Kernan

NOW YOU KNOW

- The Battle of the Coral Sea was fought entirely by warplanes.
- American dive-bombers destroyed the heart of the Japanese Navy at Midway.
- The Battle of Midway marked the turning of the tide in the war in the Pacific.

The Battle for New Guinea

IN JULY 1942, JAPANESE TROOPS LANDED IN NORTHEASTERN NEW GUINEA (part of present-day Papua New Guinea). They had already invaded outlying islands of New Guinea in January. The Japanese wanted to capture the Australian base of Port Moresby on the south coast of New Guinea. Port Moresby was about 500 miles (800 kilometers) away from Australia. The Japanese had tried to capture the port by sea, but they were halted at the Battle of the Coral Sea. The Japanese then landed troops in an attempt to reach Port Moresby by land, across the rugged, jungle-covered mountains using a small trail—the Kokoda Track. Allied troops—mostly Australian—met the Japanese in a fierce battle, pushing the Japanese back. An Allied force led by General MacArthur then attacked Japanese positions along New Guinea's north coast.

▶ In July 1942, despite their defeat at Midway, the Japanese still believed they could expand their empire. They did not, however, expect to defeat the United States. They intended to create a defensive position so strong that the Americans would lose their will to fight.

▼ Australians manning an antiaircraft gun in the village of Lae, New Guinea. The Battle of New Guinea was fought mostly by Australians.

In order to force Britain to *submit* [give in] and the United States to lose its will to fight, we shall continue expanding from the areas we have already gained . . . working long-term to establish an *impregnable* [impossible to conquer] *strategic* [strong] position, we shall actively *seize* [take] whatever opportunities for attack may occur.

from a Japanese military conference, 1942

3

I have seen men standing knee deep in the mud of a narrow mountain track, looking with complete despair at yet another seemingly insurmountable [impossible to climb] ridge. Ridge after ridge, ridge after ridge, heart breaking, hopeless, futile [useless] country.

Captain F. Piggin

◀ A 1942 letter by an Australian soldier describes conditions along the Kokoda Track. Jungle, mountains, and heavy rains made the New Guinea campaign a terrible experience for both sides. Tropical diseases were harder on the troops than the combat.

▼ Japanese soldiers killed in battle at Buna, New Guinea. Allied forces took Buna, Japan's foothold on eastern New Guinea, in December 1942. The Japanese fought to the death and suffered heavy casualties.

4

NOW YOU KNOW

- Japan invaded northeastern New Guinea in July 1942.
- Australian troops stopped the Japanese along the Kokoda Track.
- Allied troops defeated the Japanese in northeastern New Guinea in late 1942.

The Battle for Guadalcanal

BEFORE THE JAPANESE INVADED NORTHEASTERN NEW GUINEA, they began building an airstrip on nearby Guadalcanal, the largest of the Solomon Islands, northeast of Australia. U.S. intelligence received reports on this airstrip in June 1942. On Aug. 7, 1942, U.S. Marines attacked Guadalcanal and soon seized the airstrip, renamed Henderson Field after Lofton Henderson (1903-1942), a Marine flyer killed at Midway. Violent land, air, and sea battles were fought over Guadalcanal. The Japanese failed several times to retake Henderson Field and finally left the island by February 1943. The Allied victory kept open the shipping lanes between Australia and the United States.

1

We went up on the [transport ship] *Crescent City* . . . the landing craft didn't have ramps. They went in so far and then you jumped out into the water and everything had to be passed by hand. We went down the cargo nets into the *Higgins boats* [wooden 36-foot landing craft for infantry]. When we got on the beach we had to take our gear off, lay it on the beach, and form a line to pass supplies.

Louis Ortega

▲ U.S. Marine Louis Ortega remembers the landing at Guadalcanal in an interview with a historian. The operation there was one of the earliest Allied *amphibious operations*—that is, military operations by combined naval, air, and land forces for the purpose of seizing a beach or coastal area. Amphibious operations are generally considered the most complex form of warfare.

▼ In a 1942 diary entry, U.S. Marine Private James Donahue describes the jungle and its effect on servicemen.

2

The jungle is thick. . . . It took 3 days to go 6 miles [10 kilometers]. . . . The second day was murder. . . . The second night it rained and the bugs were terrible. We lay in the foxholes [shallow pits] for 13 to 14 hours at a clip and keep firing at the Japs in the jungle . . . . The mosquitoes are very bad at night. The ants & fleas bother us continually. The planes strafed [attacked with gunfire] the beach today. . . . I am very hard hit with dysentery [an illness that causes diarrhea] having had it now for 15 days. . . . By the time I get to sleep I am a nervous wreck. The Islands abound with rats, lizards. . . . At night the sound is multiplied hundreds of times so you don't know whether a Jap is around or not.

Pvt. James Donahue

3

▲ Exhausted U.S. troops wait to be taken from Guadalcanal after months of intense fighting. Thick jungle surrounds this clearing.

NOW YOU KNOW

- On Aug. 7, 1942, U.S. Marines attacked the Japanese on Guadalcanal.
- The fighting centered around a new airstrip, named Henderson Field by the U.S. Marines.
- After months of violent combat, the remaining Japanese pulled out by February 1943.

Japanese Propaganda

BOTH SIDES IN THE WAR IN THE PACIFIC PRODUCED *PROPAGANDA*—one-sided communication designed to influence people's thinking and actions. In Japan, the government announced victory after military victory to the people—even when the Japanese had lost the battles. In Asia, it claimed to be liberating people from Western domination. The Japanese promised other Asians that they would become partners in a "Greater East Asian Co-Prosperity Sphere." In reality, Japan's rule over other Asian countries was often cruel and violent. Japanese radio propaganda tried to weaken the morale of American troops in the Pacific. They also filled their own people with false stories of American cruelty.

◀ A Hollywood poster for the movie *Tokyo Rose* (1946). Tokyo Rose was the nickname given by U.S. soldiers to female announcers on Japanese propaganda radio. These English-speaking Japanese and Japanese-American women hosted shows presenting popular American music and, on occasion, news reports meant to discourage Allied soldiers and make them homesick. The broadcasts had little effect.

▶ Wartime matchboxes carry Japanese propaganda images and slogans. The box at left has threatening cartoon figures of U.S. President Franklin D. Roosevelt and British Prime Minister Winston Churchill (1874-1965). The other box shows the strength of the *Rising Sun* (the Japanese flag) destroying the United Kingdom and the United States.

3

The United States of America and the British Empire have in seeking their own *prosperity* [success] *oppressed* [kept down] other nations and peoples. Especially in East Asia they . . . sought to satisfy their . . . ambition of enslaving the entire region. . . .

Herein lies the cause of the present war. The countries of Greater East Asia, with a view to contributing to the cause of world peace, undertake to cooperate towards *prosecuting* [carrying out] the War of Greater East Asia to a successful conclusion, *liberating* [freeing] their region from the *yoke* [servitude] of British-American *domination* [rule].

Japanese declaration, 1943

◀ The "Joint Declaration of the Assembly of Greater East Asiatic Nations" was made from Tokyo on Nov. 5, 1943. This Japanese propaganda declaration blames the United States and United Kingdom for the war and promises peace and freedom for East Asia. In reality, Japan ruled the Asian countries it conquered with great cruelty, enslaving and murdering hundreds of thousands of people.

4

▶ An article from *Manga Nippon* magazine in October 1944 describes Americans as beasts, demons, savages, and devils. By 1944, the Japanese government could no longer pretend it was winning. Propaganda of this sort was meant to frighten the Japanese people into fighting to the death rather than surrendering.

. . . the American enemy, driven by its ambition to conquer the world, is coming to attack us, and as the breath and body odor of the beast approach . . . we draw the demon's features here. . . . Our ancestors called them *Ebisu* or savages long ago, and labeled the very first Westerners who came to our country the Southern Barbarians . . . they were "red hairs" or "hairy foreigners," and perceived as being of about as much worth as a foreign ear of corn. We in our times should *manifest* [show] comparable spirit . . . the barbaric tribe of Americans are devils in human skin who come from the West, we should call them *Saibanki*, or Western Barbarian Demons.

Manga Nippon, 1944

NOW YOU KNOW

- Propaganda is one-sided communication designed to influence people's thinking and actions.
- Japanese propaganda *demonized* [represented as evil] their enemies and exaggerated Japan's successes.
- The Japanese pretended to be friendly liberators, when they were often cruel conquerors.

American Propaganda

PROPAGANDA IN THE UNITED STATES WAS USUALLY MORE TRUTHFUL—about the war situation, at least—than was Japanese propaganda. U.S. propaganda used both victories and defeats to inspire the American public. However, movies, songs, radio broadcasts, and posters from the United States often did demonize the Japanese, suggesting that they were evil and less than human. American-made propaganda directed at Japanese-occupied countries was also successful at influencing opinion, as people in those nations lived under harsh Japanese rule. Attempts to convince the Japanese of America's good intentions were not as successful. Believing their own government, most Japanese soldiers—and many civilians—committed suicide or fought to the death instead of surrendering.

▶ Most of the violence and destruction in World War II occurred outside of the United States. A wartime poster shows a German-Japanese monster tearing out the Statue of Liberty in New York Harbor. The Japanese monster is meant to represent Japan's Prime Minister, Hideki Tojo, who was often used in anti-Japanese propaganda images. A tool labeled "Production" threatens the monster. The poster urges Americans to work hard producing items to defeat the Axis powers.

Stop this monster that stops at nothing... PRODUCE to the limit!

This is YOUR war!

2

Before using this bomb to destroy every resource of the military by which they are prolonging this useless war, we ask that you now petition the emperor to end the war. Our president has outlined for you the thirteen consequences of an honorable surrender. We urge that you accept these consequences and begin the work of building a new, better and peace-loving Japan. You should take steps now to cease military resistance. Otherwise, we shall *resolutely* [firmly] employ this bomb and all our other superior weapons to promptly and forcefully end the war.

A message on leaflets dropped by American forces on Japanese cities on around Aug. 6, 1945

◄ A leaflet dropped over Japan by U.S. aircraft in 1945 warns the Japanese to evacuate cities targeted for bombing. The leaflet was also propaganda, showing its readers that the Japanese armed forces were so helpless that the U.S. Air Force could name its targets in advance.

3

▶ The Hollywood movie *Guadalcanal Diary* was released in 1943, not long after the Allied victory in the battle for Guadalcanal. The poster shows soldiers in action, but much of the movie focuses on the characters' backgrounds and earlier lives in the United States. As a result, American audiences felt a direct connection with the men fighting in the Pacific.

NOW YOU KNOW

- Propaganda in the United States was often more truthful about the war situation than Japanese propaganda.
- U.S. propaganda urged Americans to work hard, while depicting the enemy as a monster.
- Hollywood war movies were effective propaganda used to inspire civilians on the home front.

Australia at War

AUSTRALIA HAD BEEN AT WAR WITH GERMANY SINCE 1939 BECAUSE OF ITS TIES to the United Kingdom. Australia formally declared war on Japan the day after the Japanese attack on Pearl Harbor in 1941 (December 8 in the United States, but December 9 in Australia). American forces soon arrived to help to defend Australia and the southwest Pacific. In July 1942, the Japanese attacked Australian territory in New Guinea (see pages 24-25) and drove toward Port Moresby on the southern coast. After brutal fighting along the Kokoda Track, Australian forces pushed back the Japanese in New Guinea. The Australians also defeated the Japanese at Milne Bay in eastern New Guinea in September 1942. Australian troops and warships fought in many areas around the Pacific.

◀ Wreckage of an American bomber plane inside a Darwin *hangar* (storage area for planes) destroyed in a raid. On Feb. 19, 1942, Japanese aircraft bombed Port Darwin in northern Australia, killing more than 200 people. It was the first of many air raids on the northern Australian port, a center for Allied shipping and supplies.

▶ An address to the Australian people from their prime minister, John Curtin (1885-1945), in the Melbourne *Herald*. The United Kingdom—fighting for its own survival—could not protect Australia against a Japanese invasion. Curtin saw the need to develop a close relationship with the United States to help defend against Japan.

Without any *inhibitions* [holding back] of any kind, I make it quite clear that Australia looks to America, free of any *pangs* [pains] as to our traditional links or kinship with the United Kingdom. We know . . . that Australia can go and Britain still hold on. We are, therefore, determined that Australia shall not go, and we will *exert* [put to use] all our energies towards shaping a plan, with the United States as the *keystone* [central part], giving Australia some confidence in being able to hold out until the tide of battle swings against the enemy.

Prime Minister John Curtin
The Herald, Dec. 27, 1941

▶ A wartime poster emphasizes the links between Australia and Britain. Animals symbolize the two countries: the Australian kangaroo and the British bulldog. Together, they tackle a Japanese soldier. The Australian flag (left corner) and British flag (right corner) are shown at the top.

We were helped . . . by a cheering piece of news . . . of which, as a *morale* [attitude] raiser, I made great use. . . . Australian troops had, at Milne Bay in New Guinea, inflicted on the Japanese their first undoubted defeat on land. If the Australians . . . had done it, so could we. Some of us may forget that of all the Allies it was Australian soldiers who first broke the spell of the *invincibility* [inability to be beaten beaten] of the Japanese Army; those of us who were in Burma have cause to remember.

General William Slim

◀ In his book *Defeat Into Victory* (1956), British General William Slim (1891-1970), the British commander who retook Burma in 1945, writes of the inspiring effect of the Australian success at Milne Bay. Japan's early victories had made them seem unstoppable. The Australian victories in New Guinea showed this to be untrue and greatly encouraged the Allies.

NOW YOU KNOW

- Australia formally declared war on Japan the day after the Japanese attack on Pearl Harbor.
- Australia turned to the United States for help in defending against the Japanese.
- Australian victories in New Guinea inspired the other Allies.

Island-Hopping

IN AUGUST 1942, THE AMERICAN INVASION OF GUADALCANAL (see pages 26-27) began a long Allied advance across the Pacific toward Japan. To cross huge stretches of ocean, the Americans adopted an "island-hopping" strategy using amphibious invasions—seaborne operations that involved combined naval, air, and land forces. Each island the Allies captured provided a base from which to strike the next target. But rather than capture every island, the Americans by-passed Japanese strongholds and invaded islands that were weakly held. The strategy stranded Japanese soldiers behind battle lines. The fighting for each island was terrible and bloody. Island-hopping carried the Allies across the Gilbert, Marshall, Caroline, and Mariana islands in the Pacific.

▶ In *Tarawa: The Story of a Battle* (1944), American war correspondent Robert Sherrod (1909-1994) describes the American landing on Tarawa in the Gilbert Islands in November 1943. Because of lower than expected tides, landing craft were stuck far from shore on reefs, and the Marines had to wade through deep water, taking heavy casualties. It was a bloody beginning to the island-hopping campaign, but valuable lessons were learned that saved lives in future invasions.

1

The 15 of us—I think it was 15—scurried over the side of the amphtrack [landing craft] into the water that was neck-deep. We started wading. No sooner had we hit the water than the Jap machine guns really opened up on us. There must have been five or six of these machine guns concentrating their fire on us. . . . It was painfully slow, wading in such deep water. And we had seven hundred yards [640 meters] to walk slowly into that machine-gun fire. . . . I was scared, as I had never been scared before.

Robert Sherrod

2

◀ U.S. Marines, pinned down behind sandbags on Tarawa, a group of tiny islands that made up a part of the Gilbert Islands. The fighting on Tarawa cost the lives of some 5,000 Japanese and almost 1,000 Marines.

3

Bear in mind the fact that to be captured means not only that you disgrace yourself, but your parents and family will never be able to hold up their heads again. Always save the last bullet for yourself.

Japanese field manual

◀ A World War II Japanese *field manual* (instruction book) makes it clear that soldiers were expected to die rather than surrender.

ISLANDS OF THE PACIFIC   **PINPOINT BATTLEFRONTS**

4

▶ A wartime map shows the military situation in the Pacific on Aug. 29, 1942. At that time, the United States faced a tough road to Japan, across the Pacific Ocean, which held many islands under Japanese control.

NOW YOU KNOW

- To cross vast expanses of ocean, the Americans adopted an "island-hopping" strategy.
- The strategy was to "hop" over many Japanese-held islands.
- The battle for Tarawa was a bloody beginning to the island-hopping campaign.

The Marianas

THE MARIANA ISLANDS PRESENTED A GREAT OPPORTUNITY for U.S. forces—and a great danger for Japan. American B-29 bombers launched from the Marianas could bomb Japanese cities—including Tokyo. Desperate to keep the Marianas, the Japanese built up their defenses and increased the numbers of troops stationed there. Eager to take the islands, the United States put together a large invasion force. On June 15, 1944, the United States began its fight for the Marianas with the Battle of Saipan. At sea, the Japanese tried to stop the U.S. Pacific Fleet around the Marianas. The Japanese were crushed there in the Battle of the Philippine Sea on June 19 and 20. By August 1944, the Marianas fell to the Americans, but at great cost to both sides. The victory, however, allowed the Americans to build five major airfields on the Mariana Islands, from which U.S. planes rained down bombs on Japan.

▼ Six-wheeled DUKW—called "Ducks"—cruised through the water and then drove right up onto the beach, delivering men and supplies. Such amphibious craft were used in the Marianas. They were one of many examples of specialized invasion equipment developed by the United States.

2

Many Japs, both military and civilians, committed suicide. It was sad to see children struggling with their parents pleading not to be thrown off the cliffs—"Please father, do not kill me. I do not want to die!" . . . One group was about 200 yards [180 meters] away from us. . . . The people look down at the rocks below and see their friends moaning down there. Just about then one of them grabs an infant and tosses him off. That seems to have been a signal because they all start jumping off. In a couple of minutes it's all over. The whole bunch lies down below either dead or dying.

War Times Journal

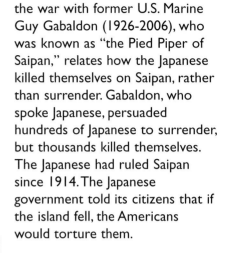

◀ An interview published after the war with former U.S. Marine Guy Gabaldon (1926-2006), who was known as "the Pied Piper of Saipan," relates how the Japanese killed themselves on Saipan, rather than surrender. Gabaldon, who spoke Japanese, persuaded hundreds of Japanese to surrender, but thousands killed themselves. The Japanese had ruled Saipan since 1914. The Japanese government told its citizens that if the island fell, the Americans would torture them.

3

▶ In *Battle Cry* (1953), American novelist Leon Uris (1924-2003) tells the story of a tough Marine sergeant named Mac. Uris was a Marine during World War II and served in the Pacific. This passage relates Mac's thoughts of panic as he goes ashore—and into battle—on Saipan.

Crouched up front, a sudden paralyzing thought shot through my mind. These might be my last minutes on earth. Another ten minutes might find me dead. As the boat dropped I caught a glimpse of the treetops . . . and I was struck with a vision of a cross on the coral shore with my name on it. I got *queasy* [a sick feeling] all over and for a moment wanted to jump out into the water and get away. I felt the palms of my hands sweat and wiped them against my *dungarees* [coarse cotton trousers] just in time to catch a *deluge* [flood] of salt water down the back of my neck.

Leon Uris

NOW YOU KNOW

- The Mariana Islands were important because the United States needed a base from which American bombers could attack Japan.
- The Japanese failed to stop the U.S. Pacific Fleet in the Battle of the Philippine Sea.
- Many Japanese civilians on Saipan killed themselves rather than surrender.

The Battle of Leyte Gulf

O N OCT. 20, 1944, AMERICAN TROOPS BEGAN TO POUR ASHORE on the Philippine Islands. In a desperate attempt to stop the invasion, the Japanese Navy attacked the U.S. Navy in the largest sea battle in history: the Battle of Leyte Gulf (October 23 through October 26). The Japanese sent some 60 ships against around 200 American and 2 Australian ships. The Americans had about 30 aircraft carriers against the Japanese, who had 4. The huge U.S. victory left Japan's navy virtually destroyed. More than 10,000 Japanese sailors and aviators died at Leyte Gulf, compared with around 3,000 Allied servicemen.

▶ In questioning by the U.S. Navy in November 1945, Admiral Soemu Toyoda (1885-1957), the commander in chief of Japan's Combined Fleet, tells of the importance of oil supplies to Japan's war effort.

I sent an order from the Combined Fleet . . . advance even though the [Japanese] fleet should be completely lost . . . should we lose in the Philippines . . . the shipping lane to the south would be completely cut off so that the fleet . . . could not obtain its fuel supply. . . . There would be no sense in saving the fleet at the expense of the loss of the Philippines.

Admiral Soemu Toyoda

▼ An aerial view of the Japanese battleship *Yamato* under attack by U.S. bombers. During the Battle of Leyte Gulf, *Yamato* sank two U.S. ships. However, for most of the war in the Pacific, air power was more important than heavily armed warships. At Leyte, planes from aircraft carriers sank *Yamato's* sister ship *Musashi*. *Yamato* itself was sunk off Okinawa in April 1945.

3

> Finally, the Commander Third Fleet can confidently report that this action and the brilliant operations of the Seventh Fleet resulted in (a) utter failure of the Japanese plan to prevent the re-occupation of the Philippines, (b) the crushing defeat of the Japanese Fleet, and (c) the elimination of serious naval threat to our operations for many months, if not forever.
>
> Admiral William F. Halsey

◀ In a report to naval commanders made after the Battle of Leyte Gulf, U.S. Navy Admiral William F. Halsey, Jr. (1882-1959), sums up the results of the battle. The Japanese navy was virtually destroyed.

4

▶ The Oct. 26, 1944, *Los Angeles Times* reports on the American victory at Leyte Gulf. The news of the battle's successful end was released immediately in the United States, and its importance was understood at once.

NOW YOU KNOW

- Desperate to save the Philippines from invasion, the Japanese attacked the U.S. Navy at Leyte Gulf.
- The Battle of Leyte Gulf was the largest sea battle in history.
- In the battle, the Japanese Navy was virtually destroyed.

Philippines Liberated

AMERICAN TROOPS FIGHTING UNDER GENERAL DOUGLAS MACARTHUR landed on the island of Leyte in the central Philippines on Oct. 20, 1944. The Japanese on Leyte held out against these forces until the end of 1944. On Jan. 9, 1945, MacArthur's forces landed on the main Philippine island, Luzon. The Japanese commander on Luzon, General Tomoyuki Yamashita (1885-1946), fought a deadly defensive campaign. By May 1945, the United States was in control, but the remaining Japanese troops on Luzon—50,000 of them— pulled back to the mountains and went on fighting until the war ended.

1

I told the President he could never justify releasing a bunch of Chinese in Formosa and abandoning a lot of Filipinos in Luzon. We had been thrown out of Luzon at the point of a bayonet and we should regain our *prestige* [reputation] by throwing the Japanese out at the point of a bayonet.

General Douglas MacArthur

◀ General Douglas MacArthur describes how he persuaded President Roosevelt to support his plan to invade the Philippines. The U.S. Navy had preferred a plan to skip the Philippines and seize Formosa (Taiwan).

▼ General MacArthur (center, with sunglasses) wades ashore on Oct. 20, 1944, as Allied forces land on Leyte. The exiled Philippine president, Sergio Osmeña (1878-1961), at far left, accompanies MacArthur. With this landing, MacArthur kept his promise of March 1942: "I shall return."

2

3

Your situation is hopeless—your defeat *inevitable* [bound to happen]. I offer you an honorable surrender. If you decide to accept, raise a large Filipino flag over the Red Cross flag now flying and send an unarmed *emissary* [messenger] with a white flag to our lines. This must be done within four hours or I am coming in. In the event you do not accept my offer, I *exhort* [urge] you that, true to the spirit of Bushido and the code of the Samurai, you permit all civilians to evacuate the Intramuros by the Victoria Gate without delay in order that no innocent blood be shed.

General Oscar Griswold

◀ On Feb. 16, 1945, U.S. Army Fourteenth Corps commander General Oscar Griswold (1886-1959) asked for the surrender of the Japanese defending the Intramuros, a walled section of Manila. The Japanese ignored the invitation. Griswold also tried to appeal to *Bushido*—traditional Japanese warrior values—to save civilian lives, but without success.

▶ U.S. tanks enter the Philippine capital, Manila, on Feb. 4, 1945. More than 10,000 Japanese troops defended Manila. Street-by-street battles followed, and much of Manila was destroyed. American casualties were high, and nearly 100,000 Philippine civilians died—many murdered by the Japanese in an event known as the Manila Massacre. Only a few hundred Japanese survived. This was the only time in the war in the Pacific that U.S. troops stormed a city.

4

NOW YOU KNOW

- General MacArthur kept his famous promise, "I shall return."
- American troops took control of the Philippines, but 50,000 Japanese held out in the mountains until the end of the war.
- Nearly 100,000 Philippine civilians were killed in the battle for Manila.

Kamikaze Pilots

IN OCTOBER 1944, JAPAN BEGAN TO USE A DANGEROUS NEW WEAPON—the *kamikaze*, or suicide pilot. *Kamikaze* means *divine wind*, and the word originally referred to a *typhoon* (storm) that destroyed a fleet sent by the Chinese Mongol ruler Kublai Khan (1215-1294) to conquer Japan in 1281. Kamikaze pilots were trained to crash their planes filled with explosives into Allied warships. The first large-scale kamikaze attacks occurred at the Battle of Leyte Gulf (see pages 38-39). By the end of the war, kamikazes had flown about 2,500 suicide missions. They sank at least 30 ships and damaged more than 350 others. By late 1944, the Allied forces had become so strong that the kamikaze attacks had little impact.

1

April 23, 1945. Twenty-three years of life are approaching their end. I do not feel as though I am about to die tomorrow. Here I am, in this far-off country, but I cannot bring myself to believe that the sole reason for this is that I must attack the enemy fleet by hurling myself against their guns and their aircraft. . . .

April 24, 1945. In a nearby room they are being rather rowdy and drinking spirits. They probably have the right idea. Personally, I prefer to wait for death quietly. I am anxious to behave well up to the last moment . . .

Ichijima Yasuo

◀ The diary of 23-year-old kamikaze pilot Ichijima Yasuo (1923-1945) shows the influence of Japanese ideas of duty and proper behavior. Ichijima died shortly after writing these entries in a suicide attack on U.S. ships off Okinawa.

2

▶ A kamikaze ties on a headband bearing the rising sun symbol of Japan before taking off on a suicide mission.

3

January 9 . . . at 6:30 a Jap plane strafed [flew low over enemy positions and attacked with machine-gun fire] our ship and crash-dived a nearby destroyer escort . . . .

January 10 . . . About 7 a.m. a few Jap planes came over. . . . One crashed into one of our ships . . . .

January 11 . . . a lone Jap plane gave us more trouble and almost crash-dived our ship . . . .

January 12 . . . It is pretty foggy and a couple of Jap planes are flying low over our formation. This almost drives a man batty [crazy], waiting for something you don't want and don't know when you are going to get it.

Bernard R. Yohe

◀ In a diary entry, a sailor describes the kamikaze attacks and the effect they had on servicemen's nerves.

▼ The flight deck of the U.S. aircraft carrier *Intrepid* on Nov. 25, 1944. Firefighters try to put out fires caused by two kamikaze strikes. Kamikazes hit the *Intrepid* on three separate occasions, but the carrier never went out of action.

4

NOW YOU KNOW

- The kamikaze was a Japanese suicide pilot.
- The goal of the kamikaze was to crash his plane into an Allied ship, causing it to sink.
- By late 1944, the Allied forces were too strong for kamikaze attacks to affect the outcome of the war.

The Brutality of War

WAR IS ALWAYS BRUTAL. THE WAR IN THE PACIFIC WAS PARTICULARLY SAVAGE. Japanese soldiers were often encouraged to behave violently by their superiors, and according to the Japanese honor code, surrender was shameful. Japanese troops almost always fought to the death, causing extremely high casualties. Wounded Japanese often attacked Allied personnel who tried to help them, while many faked surrender only to detonate an explosive among Allied troops. The Japanese also treated Allied prisoners of war with great cruelty. Prisoners were beaten, tortured, forced to work until they dropped, subjected to horrific medical experiments, or executed. The Americans, in turn, often took out their frustration and fears upon the Japanese, killing them without hesitation. Each side learned to fear and hate the other.

1

We found a body. . . . He was an American. . . . His feet were badly cut about. But worst of all was the fact that [he] was pinned to the ground with a sharp wooden stake driven through each shoulder. . . . We . . . quickly buried him in a shallow grave at the foot of a tree. The Fijians worked in grim silence but as we moved away again one of my corporals said to me: "No more prisoners, turaga [chief]." I agreed with him.

T. E. Dorman

◀ A diary entry published after the war, written by New Zealander T. E. Dorman (1914-). Dorman served with a Fijian regiment on Bougainville, New Guinea, during the war. The cruel death of an American soldier made both Dorman and his Fijian corporal determined to kill—not capture—every Japanese they met. Many Allied servicemen shared this attitude.

2

▶ A diary entry by Tom Forsyth (1910-), a Canadian in a prison camp in Niigata, in northwest Japan, details torture that happened in the camp. Many Allied prisoners of war kept secret diaries hidden from their Japanese captors. After the war, a number of prisoners' diaries were used as evidence when Japanese camp commanders and guards were put on trial for war crimes.

Atrocities [horrible criminal acts] in 5B [a POW camp in Niigata, Japan] . . . which I personally witnessed. I saw two men, Tetman, an American, and Mortimer of the Royal Rifles, tied to stakes one evening in midwinter, snow on the ground, clad only in shirt and trousers, barefooted, bareheaded, hands behind their backs, about 6 feet [1.8 meters] of slack rope to let them run around the pole which they did all night to keep from freezing.

Tom Forsyth

▲ Starving American prisoners of war in March 1945, just after their liberation from Bilibid prison in the Philippines. Thousands of Allied prisoners in different part of Asia were in similar shape. Of the many thousands of American, Australian, British, and Canadian troops taken prisoner by the Japanese, nearly 30 percent died. The death rate for Asian prisoners of the Japanese was much higher.

NOW YOU KNOW

• The war in the Pacific was fought with particular brutality.

• Japanese cruelty and ferocity made the Allied response harsher.

• Nearly 30 percent of Western Allied prisoners of war died in Japanese hands.

Civilian Suffering

CIVILIANS SUFFERED GREATLY DURING THE WAR IN THE PACIFIC. Air raids and artillery killed and injured innocent people in China and on the Pacific islands—nearly everywhere soldiers fought on land. Many people in China, India, and Southeast Asia starved to death as fighting ruined crops and stopped the exchange of goods. Japanese soldiers often mistreated civilians under their rule, using them for slave labor to build railways, roads, and bridges. Women were sometimes forced to become slaves for Japanese troops. On several occasions, the Japanese mass-murdered Chinese, Philippine, and other civilians. Many Allied civilians who worked in East Asia were also imprisoned and mistreated by the Japanese. Near the war's end, Japanese civilians endured terrible suffering and death from Allied bombings. In World War II, more civilians died than soldiers. The number of soldiers who died during the war was about 20 million. Experts believe 30 million to 40 million civilians died because of the war.

1

> The kindlier the Chinese are treated, the more demanding and *impudent* [rude] they become. Therefore, neither generosity nor *leniency* [mercy] are necessary. . . . Reduce the food ration of those who do not work effectively. . . . Bathing facilities are unnecessary because according to Chinese tradition they are offered by the defeated to the victors.
>
> Japanese instructions for treating prisoners

◀ The Japanese government gives orders that Chinese brought to Japan to work in a mine be mistreated. The Japanese regarded the Chinese as less than human. Racist attitudes of this kind were common during the war.

2

▶ A message sent by Marlovi Haddi, an Allied sympathizer, to Allied guerilla forces left behind to fight after the fall of Burma. The message shows the danger of being in a combat zone. It also testifies to the brave willingness of some civilians to suffer for the promise of liberation and freedom.

> *Honourable Sir and Captain, last week I asked you to be bombing X—I give the positions of the Jap nicely. The bombing man comes and makes very bad bombings. . . . They kill my big son and his two wives and they kill my brother. . . . Please tell the bombing man to come again, but now to bomb nicely. For which I ever pray and successful British come quickly to ease the terrible sufferings of the [people].*
>
> Marlovi Haddi

▼ Chinese workers in 1940 remove civilians killed by a Japanese air raid on Chongqing (then Chunking), in central China. The dead were buried in a mass grave. In wartime, it was sometimes difficult to identify the dead and give each person a separate burial. The bodies were too injured and too numerous.

3

NOW YOU KNOW

- Civilians suffered greatly from air raids and fighting in the war in the Pacific.
- The Japanese often treated civilians very badly.
- More civilians died in the war than soldiers.

The War in Asia

THE BATTLES IN MAINLAND AND SOUTHEAST ASIA WERE often described as "forgotten wars." Because they were so far away from Europe and the United States and so unfamiliar to Western people, they were not always reported on in Western newspapers. But these conflicts were long and violent. Early in the war, Japan took much of eastern and southern China, conquered Burma (now Myanmar) and Malaya (a region of modern Malaysia), and ruled Thailand and Indochina (Cambodia, Laos, and Vietnam). In March 1944, the Japanese invaded India, but the Allies pushed them back and began a slow recovery of Southeast Asia. The war in China was still undecided when Japan surrendered in September 1945.

▶ A February 1945 newspaper reports the reopening of a supply road between Burma and China earlier in 1945. The Japanese had closed the Burma Road (see page 18)—the Allies' overland supply route to China—in April 1942.

▼ British soldiers during the battle for Kohima in northeast India in 1944. Both the Allies and the Japanese struggled with exhaustion and disease as they fought in the jungles of Asia.

1

KUNMING, CHINA Firecrackers roared like a hundred machine guns down Kunming's jammed streets where hundreds of thousands turned out to greet the arrival of the first overland *convoy* [group of trucks] into China. . . . the *cavalcade* [procession] of 113 vehicles decked in flags and *bunting* [patriotic decorations] moved slowly between packed lanes. Children, students, soldiers and the massed common people of Kunming, their faces alight with . . . joy over a spectacle that *symbolized* [stood for] . . . the end of China's isolation.

China Command Post, 1945

2

▶ U.S. Army General Joseph Stilwell (1883-1946) recalls his struggles with Chinese leader Chiang Kai-shek (1887-1975). Stilwell was commander of the American forces in China, Burma, and India. His words reflected American impatience with Chiang's lack of aggression in fighting the Japanese. But, Chiang's forces had already sustained heavy losses in 1937, and he feared the armies of the Chinese Communists.

3

I have never heard [Chinese leader] Chiang Kai-shek say a single thing that *indicated* [showed] gratitude to the President or to our country for the help we were extending to him. *Invariably* [always], when anything was promised, he would want more. . . . He would complain that the Chinese had been fighting for six or seven years and yet we gave them practically nothing. It would of course be *undiplomatic* [lacking in skill for handling sensitive matters] to go into the nature of the military effort Chiang Kai-shek had made since 1938. It was practically zero.

General Joseph Stilwell

4

◀ Troops of the Communist Chinese 8th Army guard China's famous Great Wall. The Communists and Chiang Kai-shek's Nationalists were bitter enemies, but both sides fought the Japanese. As the Allies neared victory over Japan, however, both Communists and Nationalists avoided clashes with the Japanese. They would soon fight a bitter civil war, for which they were saving troops and supplies.

NOW YOU KNOW

• The "forgotten wars" in Asia were fought in mainland and Southeast Asia.

• The Burma Road was an important route for military supplies for China.

• After the Japanese surrender, Chinese Nationalists and Communists resumed their civil war for control of China.

Bombing Japan

UNTIL LATE IN THE WAR, JAPAN WAS FAIRLY SAFE FROM ALLIED BOMBING. It was too far away to be bombed by planes of that time. That changed when the Americans took the Mariana Islands (see pages 36-37) and built airfields. Bombing raids on Japan started in November 1944. The raids became more intense and destructive after Air Force Major General Curtis LeMay (1906-1990) took charge in January 1945. B-29 bombers flew over Japan under cover of night, dropping huge quantities of *incendiary* (fire-causing) bombs that burned Japan's cities, killing hundreds of thousands of civilians. The country was in ruins, yet Japan's rulers refused to surrender.

▶ In a diary entry, American B-29 pilot Robert Ramer (1922-) describes a bombing in 1945, as he flew into an already-ruined Tokyo to drop even more incendiaries. By the time Japan surrendered in August 1945, its cities had been destroyed and its industries shattered. Millions of its citizens were killed, injured, or homeless.

1

Suddenly, way off at about 2 o'clock [the pilot is using the position of a clock's hour hand to describe a position in the sky], I saw a glow on the horizon like the sun rising or maybe the moon. The whole city of Tokyo was below us stretching from wingtip to wingtip, ablaze in one enormous fire with yet more fountains of flame pouring down from the B-29s. The black smoke billowed up thousands of feet, causing powerful thermal [heat] currents that buffeted [knocked about] our plane severely, bringing with it the horrible smell of burning flesh.

Robert Ramer

2

Roofs collapsed under the bombs' impact and within minutes the *frail* [weak] houses of wood and paper were aflame, lighted from the inside like paper lanterns. The hurricane-force wind puffed up great *clots* [lumps] of flame and sent burning planks . . . through the air to *fell* [knock down] people and set fire to what they touched. Flames from a distant cluster of houses would suddenly spring up close at hand, traveling at the speed of a forest fire. Then screaming families abandoned their homes; sometimes the women had already left, carrying their babies and dragging crates or mattresses. Too late: the circle of fire had closed off their street. Sooner or later, everyone was surrounded by fire.

Robert Guillain

◀ In *I Saw Tokyo Burning* (1981), French journalist Robert Guillain (1908-1998) describes a firebombing of Tokyo on the night of March 9 through the morning of March 10, 1945. Many Japanese buildings were partly or completely made of wood and paper, so incendiary bombs were very destructive. Entire city blocks exploded in flames. Guillain had been trapped in Japan after Pearl Harbor and spent the war there.

▲ The docks of the Japanese city of Kobe during a raid by some 500 B-29 airplanes in June 1945, from an aerial photograph taken from a U.S. bomber. Thick smoke blots out most of the city. Below the airplane, more bombs are falling.

NOW YOU KNOW

- B-29 bombers devastated Japanese cities with incendiary bombs.
- Because many Japanese buildings were made of wood and paper, fires spread quickly.
- Despite the destruction and loss of life, Japan refused to surrender.

Iwo Jima

THE ISLAND-HOPPING STRATEGY BROUGHT THE AMERICANS to Iwo Jima (now Iwo To), a tiny volcanic island only 750 miles (1,207 kilometers) from Japan. On Feb. 19, 1945, U.S. Marines hit the island's black-sand beaches. Iwo Jima was defended by some 21,000 Japanese troops prepared to fight to the death from miles of hidden tunnels, thousands of hidden caves, and concrete bunkers. The fighting was difficult—at times the Marines would fight all day to gain 100 yards (90 meters). The American flag was raised on Mount Suribachi on February 23, but fighting continued through March 16. Iwo Jima was the bloodiest battle in U.S. Marine Corps history, with nearly 7,000 Americans killed. Only about 200 of the Japanese defenders surrendered. The rest were either killed or committed suicide.

▶ In an interview for the British television series *The World at War* (1973), former Marine Corpsman Herman Rabeck (1923-) describes the horrors of the landing on Iwo Jima. The Japanese were well protected and well placed to fire on the Marine invaders.

▼ Wrecked American landing craft and equipment litter the volcanic-ash beach at Iwo Jima. Mount Suribachi looms in the background.

As you hit the island it was—if there's ever been hell, this was it. There wasn't a living thing anywhere in sight. I would say that forty to fifty per cent of the men I got close to were dead. I was actually hopping over bodies and you never could tell who was alive and who wasn't because everybody hit the ground and stayed there.

Herman Rabeck

3

▶ In early March 1945, Tadamichi Kuribayashi (1891-1945), the Japanese commander on Iwo Jima, radioed this farewell message to the army staff headquarters. The commander apologizes for his failure, even though he had been given a hopeless task. He is proud that his men gave their lives "without regret." Soon after this message was sent, Kuribayashi was dead.

We are sorry indeed we could not have defended the island [Iwo Jima] successfully. Now I, Kuribayashi, believe that the enemy will invade Japan proper from this island. . . . I am very sorry because I can imagine the scenes of disaster in our empire. However, I comfort myself a little, seeing my officers and men die without regret after struggling in this inch-by-inch battle against an overwhelming [crushing] enemy . . . .

Tadamichi
Kuribayashi

4

◀ *Raising the Flag on Iwo Jima,* by American photographer Joe Rosenthal (1911-2006), is one of the most famous images of the war. (This version of the photograph has been tinted; the original is black and white.) Rosenthal received the 1945 Pulitzer Prize for photography for the image.

NOW YOU KNOW

• Japanese forces had carefully prepared tunnels and caves from which to defend Iwo Jima.

• The battle for Iwo Jima was the bloodiest in U.S. Marine Corps history.

• *Raising the Flag on Iwo Jima* has become one of the most famous war photos ever taken.

The Struggle for Okinawa

AFTER IWO JIMA, THE ALLIES STRUCK THE ISLAND OF OKINAWA, just 350 miles (563 kilometers) south of the main islands of Japan. On April 1, 1945, American troops poured onto Okinawa's shore, beginning three months of brutal combat against the Japanese over steep hills and deep ravines. At sea, Japan continued to send wave after wave of kamikazes at the U.S. Navy, attacking with what remained of the Japanese fleet. By the time the Battle of Okinawa ended on June 21, dozens of U.S. ships had been sunk and hundreds damaged. The Japanese Navy lost 16 ships and thousands of aircraft. The battle took the lives of 110,000 Japanese and Okinawan troops. The Americans lost 12,500 soldiers, sailors, and aviators. About 80,000 Okinawan civilians died as well, including many who chose to kill themselves rather than be conquered. The home islands of Japan were the next Allied target.

► The April 2, 1945, edition of *The New York Times* reports the Allied landing at Okinawa. The "amazingly light" Japanese resistance was a deliberate strategy. The Japanese stayed within their strongholds, saving their strength to hold out as long as possible.

AMERICANS INVADE OKINAWA IN RYUKYUS; SEIZE 2 AIRFIELDS; FIRST RESISTANCE LIGHT

Guam, Monday, April 2—The United States Tenth Army landed yesterday morning on Okinawa . . . .

The veteran *doughboys* [infantrymen] and marines met amazingly light resistance from the minute they landed yesterday at 8:30 A.M. They pushed up the steep slopes from the landing beaches with ease, although the shore was dominated by enemy guns on high ground.

The New York Times

◄ American landing craft crowd the beach at Okinawa with support ships in the background.

54

▶ A poem written by General Isamu Cho (1895-1945), chief of staff of the Japanese army that fought in the Battle of Okinawa. When the battle was clearly lost for the Japanese, Cho wrote this, his last poem. Then he and army commander General Mitsuru Ushijima (1887-1945), killed themselves.

3

The devil *foe* [enemy] tightly grips our southwest
  land,
His aircraft fill the sky, his ships control the sea;
Bravely we fought for ninety days inside a dream;
We have used up our *withered* [dried up] lives,
But our souls race to heaven.

General Isamu Cho

▼ American tanks attack a Japanese bunker on Okinawa with flamethrowers. Flamethrowers proved to be an effective, if gruesome, way of clearing Japanese soldiers from caves and bunkers.

NOW YOU KNOW

• Okinawa was the bloodiest U.S. battle in the Pacific.

• The Japanese lost nearly 8,000 aircraft in the battle—many of which were kamikazes.

• After Okinawa, only Japan itself remained to be taken.

Hiroshima and Nagasaki

OKINAWA TAUGHT THE ALLIES A GRIM LESSON. While planning the invasion of Japan for November 1945, war experts estimated it might cost 1 million American lives—and many millions of Japanese lives. After the death of President Roosevelt in April 1945, a new U.S. president was sworn in—Harry S. Truman (1884-1972). Hoping to make the invasion of Japan unnecessary, Truman decided to use a terrifying new secret weapon: the atomic bomb. On July 26, the United States, the United Kingdom, and China issued a statement threatening to destroy Japan unless it surrendered. Japan refused. On Aug. 6, 1945, a B-29, the *Enola Gay*, dropped a single atomic bomb that devastated the Japanese city of Hiroshima. The Japanese again refused to surrender. On August 9, another bomb blasted the city of Nagasaki. More than 100,000 people were immediately killed in the two bombings. Later, thousands more died of injuries and from the effects of radiation.

▶In an interview for the British television series *The World at War* (1973), Hiroshima housewife Kishi Matsukawa recalls watching the atomic bomb explode.

▼ Hiroshima after the atomic bombing. A single bomb—and its burning winds—flattened the city.

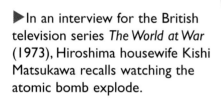

I looked up and there I saw two boxes, something like boxes hanging from a parachute and coming down.... Then in a twinkling of an eye there was a bomb burst.... When I regained consciousness ... I found that my leg was broken. I tried to speak and I found that I had lost six of my teeth.... I found my face burned and my back burned.... I crawled to the river and when I got there I saw hundreds ... floating down the river.

Kishi Matsukawa

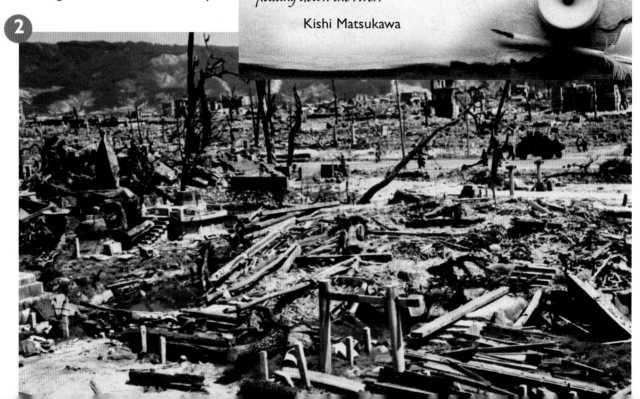

3

When the atom bombs were dropped and . . . we learned to our astonishment that we would not be obliged in a few months to rush up the beaches near Tokyo assault-firing while being machine-gunned, *mortared* [struck by mortar shells], and shelled . . . we broke down and cried with relief and joy. We were going to live. We were going to grow to adulthood after all. The killing was all going to be over, and peace was actually going to be the state of things.

Paul Fussell

◀ In a *New Republic* article published after the war, American author and historian Paul Fussell (1924-) recalls that he and his fellow soldiers were overjoyed when they heard of the atomic bombings. In 1945 Fussell was scheduled to take part in the invasion of Japan. Critics of the bombings, both in 1945 and since, have called the attacks on Hiroshima and Nagasaki war crimes against the people of Japan. President Harry S. Truman said he ordered the bombings to save the lives of 1 million American soldiers.

4

▶ An atomic bomb of the "Fat Man" type that fell on Nagasaki is displayed in a museum in Washington, D.C.

NOW YOU KNOW

- War experts estimated that the invasion of Japan would cost 1 million American lives.
- The Allies threatened to destroy Japan unless it surrendered. Japan refused.
- More than 100,000 people were immediately killed in the bombings of Hiroshima and Nagasaki.

Peace

SOME JAPANESE LEADERS STILL WANTED TO FIGHT ON, even after the bombings of Hiroshima and Nagasaki, but on Aug. 14, 1945, Emperor Hirohito urged the government to accept defeat and Japan agreed to a complete surrender. Fighting ended, and Japanese officials signed a statement of surrender on September 2. World War II was over. Japanese forces left occupied territories. American forces, commanded by General Douglas MacArthur, occupied Japan. In 1947, a new Japanese constitution transferred power from the emperor to the people. In addition, the constitution granted voting rights to women. The occupation of Japan ended in 1952. Japan became a democratic nation. It also became the United States' most constant ally in Asia.

1

We have ordered our Government to communicate to the Governments of the United States, Great Britain, China, and the Soviet Union that our Empire accepts the provisions [terms] of their joint declaration.

. . . Despite the best that has been done by everyone—the gallant [brave] fighting of the military and naval forces . . . the war situation has developed not necessarily to Japan's advantage, while the general trends of the world have all turned against her interest.

. . . it is according to the dictates of time and fate that we have resolved to pave the way for a grand peace for all the generations to come. . . .

Emperor Hirohito

◀ Emperor Hirohito broadcast news of the surrender to the Japanese people on Aug. 15, 1945. In this statement, Hirohito never uses the word *surrender*, and he makes the decision sound like an act of nobility. MacArthur protected the emperor from being accused of war crimes.

▶Chinese-Americans in New York City rejoice over the news of Japan's surrender. When people heard the news that the war had ended, they poured out into the streets to celebrate. In New York City's Times Square, 2 million people gathered for a 24-hour-long celebration.

2

▶ After the formal surrender on Sept. 2, 1945, General MacArthur broadcast a radio message to the world. Its positive tone anticipates the generous treatment of Japan that became typical of MacArthur's rule.

▼ Japanese officials and military leaders arrive on board the American battleship *Missouri* in Tokyo Bay on Sept. 2, 1945. They signed the official statement of surrender before representatives of the Allied nations. The emperor did not attend this ceremony.

3

Today the guns are silent. A great tragedy has ended. A great victory has been won. . . . As I look back on the long, *tortuous* [twisting] trail from those grim days of Bataan and Corregidor, when an entire world lived in fear, when democracy was on the defensive everywhere, when modern civilization trembled in the balance, I thank a merciful God that he has given us the faith, the courage and the power from which to mold victory. . . . We must go forward to preserve in peace what we won in war.

Gen. Douglas MacArthur

4

NOW YOU KNOW

- The emperor convinced Japanese leaders to surrender.
- Japanese troops withdrew from conquered territories, and U.S. forces occupied Japan.
- The occupation ended in 1952, and Japan became an independent democracy.

Timeline

1931 September	Japan seizes Manchuria from China.
1937 July	War breaks out between Japan and China.
1939 September	World War II begins in Europe.
1941	
December 7	Japan attacks the U.S. fleet at Pearl Harbor, Hawaii. Japan invades Southeast Asia.
December 8	The U.S., the U.K., Canada, and Australia declare war on Japan.
1942	
February 15	The Japanese capture Singapore.
February 19	The Japanese bomb Port Darwin, northern Australia.
February 27	The Japanese defeat the Allied fleet at the Battle of the Java Sea.
April 9	U.S. and Philippine troops on Bataan Peninsula surrender.
May	Japan completes its conquest of Burma.
May 4-8	The Battle of the Coral Sea prevents a Japanese attack on Port Moresby.
May 6	U.S. and Philippine troops surrender on Corregidor and throughout the Philippines.
June 4-6	The Allies defeat Japan in the Battle of Midway. (American B-17 bombers engaged the Japanese at Midway on June 3.)
August 7	U.S. Marines land on Guadalcanal.
September 7	The Japanese are defeated at Milne Bay.
1943	
February	The last Japanese troops are evacuated from Guadalcanal.
November 20	U.S. forces land on Tarawa, beginning U.S. "island-hopping" across the Central Pacific.
1944	
March 6	The Japanese invade India but are driven back.
June 19-20	A U.S. naval force defeats the Japanese in the Battle of the Philippine Sea.
July 9	U.S. forces capture Saipan.
July 18	Japanese Prime Minister Hideki Tojo resigns.
October 20	The Allies begin landing in the Philippines.
October 23-26	The Americans defeat Japan's navy in the Battle of Leyte Gulf.
1945	
January	The Burma Road, linking India with China, is reopened.
March 9-10	U.S. aircraft firebomb Tokyo, in the single most destructive raid of the war in the Pacific.
March 16	U.S. Marines capture Iwo Jima.
April 12	U.S. President Roosevelt dies, and Harry S. Truman becomes president.
May 3	The Allies capture the Burmese capital, Rangoon.
June 21	Allied forces capture Okinawa.
August 6	A U.S. B-29 drops an atomic bomb on Hiroshima, Japan.
August 8	The Soviet Union declares war on Japan.
August 9	An atomic bomb is dropped on Nagasaki, Japan.
August 15	Japan agrees to surrender unconditionally.
September 2	Japanese representatives sign surrender documents on board the U.S.S. *Missouri*.

Sources

4-5 Document 1 – The Tripartite Pact between Germany, Italy, and Japan. 27 Sept. 1940. *The Avalon Project.* Web. 5 May 2010. Document 3 – Roosevelt, Franklin Delano. Radio broadcast. 29 Dec. 1940. In *FDR's Fireside Chats.* Norman: University of Oklahoma Press, 1992. Print.

6-7 Document 2 – Durdin, F. Tillman. "Butchery Marked Capture of Nanking." *The New York Times* 18 Dec. 1937: 1+. Microfilm. Document 3 – "Freezing Statement's Text." *The New York Times* 26 July 1941: 5. Microfilm.

8-9 Document 1 – Admiral Osami Nagano. 1941. Quoted in Asada, Sadao. *From Mahan to Pearl Harbor: The Imperial Japanese Navy and the United States.* Annapolis, Md.: U.S. Naval Institute Press, 2006. Print. Document 2 – *The New York Times* 8 Dec, 1941:1. Document 3 – Roosevelt, Franklin Delano. Radio broadcast. 8 Dec. 1941. In Safire, William. *Lend Me Your Ears: Great Speeches in History.* New York: Norton, 2004. Print.

10-11 Document 2 – Nicolson, Harold G. *Diaries and Letters, 1939–45.* Ed. Nigel Nicolson. London: Collins, 1967. Print. Document 4 – Brown, Cecil. *Suez to Singapore.* New York: Random House, 1942. Print.

12-13 Document 1 – Ind, Allison. *Bataan, The Judgment Seat.* New York: Macmillan, 1944. Print. Document 3 – MacArthur, Douglas. "They Died Hard – Those Savage Men." *Time* 10 July 1964:72+. Print.

14-15 Document 2 – Dyess, William. E. *The Dyess Story.* New York: G.P. Putnam's Sons, 1944. Print. Document 3 – *The Tribune* [Manila newspaper]. 1942. Quoted in Toland, John. *The Rising Sun; The Decline and Fall of the Japanese Empire, 1936-1945.* New York: Random House, 1970. Print.

16-17 Document 1 – Bernatitus, Ann. Interview. 25 Jan. 1994. In Littleton, Mark R. *Doc: Heroic Stories of Medics, Corpsmen, and Surgeons in Combat.* St. Paul, MN: Zenith Press, 2005. Print. Document 2 – Weise, Selene H. C. *The Good Soldier.* Shippensburg, PA: Burd Street Press, 1999. Print.

18-19 Document 1 – Randle, John. Interview. Date unknown. Quoted in Max Arthur, Comp. *Forgotten Voices of World War II.* Guilford, CT: Lyons Press, 2004. Print. Document 2 – Slim, William J. *Defeat into Victory.* London: Cassell, 1956. Print.

20-21 Document 2 – "World Battlefronts: Home is the Sailor." *Time* 9 March 1942: 18-20. Print. Document 3 – Collins, J. A. "Battle of the Java Sea, 27 February, 1942." *London Gazette* 7 July 1948, supplement: 3939. *London Gazette.* Web. 5 May 2010.

22-23 Document 2 – Fuchida, Mitsuo, et al. *Midway, the Battle that Doomed Japan.* 1955. Annapolis, MD: Naval Institute Press, 2001. Print. Document 4 – Kernan, Alvin. *Crossing the Line: A Bluejacket's Odyssey in World War II.* 1994. New Haven: Yale University Press, 2007. Print.

24-25 Document 1– Japanese military conference. 1942. Quoted in Bix, Herbert P. *Hirohito and the Making of Modern Japan.* New York: HarperCollins, 2000. Print. Document 3 – Captain F. Piggin. Letter. 1942. Quoted in Johnston, Mark. *At the Front Line: Experiences of Australian Soldiers in World War II.* Cambridge University Press, 1996.

26-27 Document 1 – Ortega, Louis. "Oral History—Battle of Guadalcanal, 1942-1943." *Naval History and Heritage Command.* U.S. Navy, 2000. Web. 5 May 2010. Document 2 – Donahue, James. "Journal Entries by Pfc. James A. Donahue." *Guadalcanal Journal.* Jim Donahue, Jr., 2010. Web. 5 May 2010.

28-29 Document 3 – Joint Declaration of the Assembly of Greater East Asiatic Nations. 5 Nov. 1943. In Lu, David John. *Japan: A Documentary History.* Vol. 2. M. E. Sharpe, 1997. Print. Document 4 – Article from *Manga Nippon.* Oct. 1944. Quoted in Dower, John W. *War Without Mercy.* New York: Pantheon Books, 1986. Print.

30-31 Document 2 – "Leaflets Dropped on Cities in Japan." *American Experience: The Presidents: Harry S. Truman.* PBS, 2009. Web. 5 May 2010.

32-33 Document 2 – "Mr. Curtin's 'Melbourne Herald' Article." *Keesing's Contemporary Archives* 3 Jan. 1942: 4966. Print. Document 4 – Slim, Sir William. *Defeat Into Victory.* Cassell, 1956. Print.

34-35 Document 1 – Sherrod, Robert. *Tarawa: The Story of a Battle.* New York: Duell, Sloan and Pearce, 1944. Print. Document 3 – Japanese field manual during World War II. Quoted in Costello, John. *The Pacific War.* New York: Quill, 1982. Print.

36-37 Document 2 – "Guy Gabaldon: An Interview and Discussion." *War Times Journal,* 1998. Web. 5 May 2010. Document 3 – Uris, Leon. *Battle Cry.* New York: Putnam, 1953. Print.

38-39 Document 1– Admiral Soemu Toyoda. 1945. Quoted in United States Strategic Bombing Survey. *Interrogation of Japanese Officials.* Vol. 2. Washington, D.C.: U.S. Govt. Printing Office, 1946. Print. Document 3 – Admiral William F. Halsey. Report Made After the Battle of Leyte. Quoted in Cutler, Thomas J. *The Battle of Leyte Gulf, 23-26 October, 1944.* HarperCollins, 1994. Print.

40-41 Document 1 – General Douglas MacArthur. Quoted in General Eichelberger, Robert L., and Emma G. Eichelberger. *Dear Miss Em: General Eichelberger's War in the Pacific, 1942-1945.* Westport, CT: Greenwood Press, 1972. Print. Document 3 – General Oscar Griswold. 16 Feb. 1945. Quoted in Connaughton, R. M., John Pimlott, and Duncan Anderson. *The Battle for Manila.* London: Bloomsbury, 1995. Print.

42-43 Document 1 – Ichijima, Yasuo. Diary entry. 23 Apr. 1945. Quoted in Aldrich, Richard. *The Faraway War: Personal Diaries of the Second World War in Asia and the Pacific.* London: Doubleday, 2005. Print. Document 3 – Yohe, Bernard R. Unpublished diary. Quoted in Spector, Ronald H. *At War, At Sea: Sailors and Naval Combat in the Twentieth Century.* New York: Viking, 2001. Print.

44-45 Document 1 – Dorman, T. E. *The Green War.* Hamilton, NZ: T.E. Dorman, 1997. Print. Document 2 – Forsyth, Tom. "Tom Forsyth's Diary." *Hong Kong Veterans Commemorative Association.* HKVCA, 2010. Web. 12 May 2010.

46-47 Document 1 – Japanese instructions for treating prisoners. Sept. 1944. Quoted in Ienaga, Saburo. *The Pacific War: World War II and the Japanese, 1931-1945.* New York: Pantheon Books, 1978. Print. Document 2 – Haddi, Marlovi. Quoted in Irwin, Anthony. *Burmese Outpost.* London: Collins, 1945. Print.

48-49 Document 1 – Isaacs, Harold. "Triumphant First Convoy to Kunming Greeted by Thousands." *China Command Post* 9 Feb. 1945: n. pag. Web. 12 May 2010. Document 3 – Stilwell, Joseph W. *The Stilwell Papers.* 1948. New York: Da Capo Press, 1991. Print.

50-51 Document 1 – Ramer, Robert. Diary entry. 9 Mar. 1945. Quoted in Hastings, Max. *Retribution: The Battle for Japan, 1944-45.* New York: Alfred A. Knopf, 2008. Print. Document 2 – Guillain, Robert. *I Saw Tokyo Burning: An Eyewitness Narrative from Pearl Harbor to Hiroshima.* Garden City, NY: Doubleday, 1981. Print.

52-53 Document 1 – Rabeck, Herman. Quoted in Holmes, Richard, ed. *The World at War: The Landmark Oral History from the Previously Unpublished Archives.* London: Ebury, 2007. Print. Document 3 – Kuribayashi, Tadamichi. Quoted in Toland, John. *The Rising Sun – The Decline and Fall of the Japanese Empire, 1936-1945.* New York: Random House, 1970. Print.

54-55 Document 1 – Rae, Bruce. "Americans Invade Okinawa in Ryukyus." *The New York Times* 2 April 1945: 1+. Microfilm. Document 3– Yahara, Hiromichi. *The Battle for Okinawa.* New York: Wiley, 1997.

56-57 Document 1 – Matsukawa, Kishi. Quoted in Holmes, Richard, ed. *The World at War: The Landmark Oral History from the Previously Unpublished Archives.* London: Ebury, 2007. Print. Document 3 – Fussell, Paul. "Hiroshima: A Soldier's View." *The New Republic* 22/29 Aug. 1981: 26-30. Print.

58-59 Document 1 – Emperor Hirohito. Surrender broadcast. 15 Aug. 1945. In Lu, David John. *Japan: A Documentary History.* Vol. 2. Armonk, NY: M. E. Sharpe, 1997. Print. Document 3 – General Douglas MacArthur. Radio broadcast. 2 Sept. 1945. Available in "Holy Mission Completed, MacArthur Informs U.S." *Milwaukee Journal* 2 Sept. 1945: 1. Google News. Web. 12 May 2010.

Additional resources

Books

Angels of Mercy: The Army Nurses of World War II, by Betsy Kuhn, Atheneum, 1999

The Attack on Pearl Harbor: The United States Enters World War II (Milestones in American History series), by John C. Davenport, Chelsea House Publishers, 2009

Battling in the Pacific: Soldiering in World War II (Soldiers on the Battlefront series), by Susan Provost Beller, Lerner Publishing Group, 2008

Fighting For Honor: Japanese Americans and World War II, by Michael L. Cooper, Clarion Books, 2000

The Good Fight: How World War II Was Won, by Stephen E. Ambrose, Atheneum, 2001

Navajo Code Talkers, by Nathan Aaseng, Greenhaven Press, 2005

World War II (Opposing Viewpoints in World History series), by Don Nardo, Greenhaven Press, 2005

Websites

http://www.bbc.co.uk/history/worldwars/wwtwo
The British Broadcasting Company (BBC) created this interactive site on World War II.

http://www.nationalgeographic.com/pearlharbor
National Geographic's site on Pearl Harbor includes a multimedia map, a timeline, and listings of the ships and planes that were at Pearl Harbor on Dec. 7, 1941.

http://www.nps.gov/valr/index.htm
The U.S. National Park Service site for the U.S.S. *Arizona* Memorial contains a history section and photos.

http://www.pbs.org/wgbh/amex/macarthur/sfeature/bataan_capture.html
A site by the Public Broadcasting System (PBS) on World War II in the Philippines. It includes information on General MacArthur, the Bataan Death March, and interviews with veterans who served in the Philippines during World War II.

http://teacher.scholastic.com/activities/wwii/hiroshima/index.htm
A site recounting the story of a Japanese-American survivor of the bombing of Hiroshima.

Index

Index

Acknowledgments

AKG-Images: 1, 19 (Ullstein Bild), 40, 42 (Ullstein Bild), 49, 53 (Ullstein Bild), 55 (Ullstein Bild); Art Archive: 8, 28 (top), 28 (below), 45 (Culver Pictures), 48; Bridgeman Art Library: 22 (Private Collection), 47, 59; Corbis: 5, 12 (Bettmann), 15 (Seattle Post-Intelligencer Collection/Museum of History and Industry), 23, 31 (Michael Nicholson), 34 (Bettmann), 35 (Bettmann), 36, 43, 51, 52, 54, 56 (Bettmann), 57 (Bettmann), 58; Getty: 7 (George Rodger/Time Life Pictures), 13 (Keystone), 14 (Keystone), 24 (Myron Davis/Time & Life Pictures), 27 (Ralph Morse/Time Life Pictures), 30 (Galerie Bilderwelt), 32 (Keystone), 38 (Keystone), 41 (Mansell/Time & Life Pictures); Library of Congress: 9, 25 (U.S. Army); Mary Evans Picture Library: 11; National Women's History Museum: 17; Topfoto: 4, 6, 20, 33 (The National Archives/HIP), 39.

Cover main image: Corbis (Matthew Harris/Cordaiy Photo Library Ltd); inset image: AKG-Images